REVISED AND UPDATED

Transportation
Around the
World

Planes

Chris Oxlade

Heinemann Library
Chicago, Illinois

©2000, 2008 Heinemann Library
a division of Reed Elsevier Inc.
Chicago, Illinois

Customer Service 888-454-2279
Visit our website at www.heinemannraintree.com

Designed by Kimberly R. Miracle, Ray Hendren, Cavedweller Studio and Q2A Creative
Printed in China by South China Printing Company

12 11 10 09 08
10 9 8 7 6 5 4 3 2 1

New edition ISBN-10:   1-4329-0203-2 (hardcover)
                        1-4329-0212-1 (paperback)
New edition ISBN-13:   978-1-4329-0203-2 (hardcover)
                        978-1-4329-0212-4 (paperback)

The Library of Congress has cataloged the first edition as follows:
Oxlade, Chris.
        Planes / Chris Oxlade.
                p. cm. — (Transportation around the world)
        Includes bibliographical references and index.
Summary: Brief text and photographs explain what planes are, describe different types of planes, and examine how they developed and how they are used.
ISBN 1-57572-303-4
1.   Airplanes — Juvenile literature. [1. Airplanes.] I. Title. II. Series.

TL547. 095423 2000
629.133'34 — dc21

                                                                00-027549

Acknowledgments
The publisher would like to thank the following for permission to reproduce photographs: AirTeam Images 2007 pp. **13** (Eric Fortin), **25** (Colin Work); Alamy p. **24** (Steve Mansfield-Devine); Corbis p. **21** (George Hall); Getty Images/AFP p. **15**; Photodisc pp. **23**, **29**; Quadrant pp. **5** (Jeremy Hoare), **7** (R. Shaw), 12 (Erik Simonsen), **16** (Mark Wagner), **17** (LG Photo), **18** (Anthony R. Dalton), **19** (Paul Phelan), **22** (Tony Hobbs), **27** (Tony Hobbs); Quadrant/Flight pp. **6**, **8**, **9**, **11**, **20**, **26**; The Stock Market p. 10 (Russell Munson); Tony Stone Images pp. 14 (Alan Smith), 28 (World Perspectives); Trip p. 4 (Malcolm Fife).

Cover photograph reproduced with permission of Getty Images/Science Faction (Paul Bowen).

Every effort has been made to contact copyright holders of any material reproduced in this book. Any omissions will be rectified in subsequent printings if notice is given to the publisher.

Contents

Some words are shown in bold, **like this**. You can find out what they mean by looking in the glossary.

What Is a Plane?

A plane is a machine that flies through the air. Some planes carry passengers. Some planes carry **goods** called cargo. People often fly planes for fun.

These pilots are enjoying the open air in their private plane.

Pilots need to know how high they are and how fast they are going.

The person who flies a plane is called the **pilot**. The pilot controls the takeoff and landing and **steers** the plane through the air. Some pilots have computers to help them fly the plane.

How Planes Work

This small plane can hold about 10 passengers.

Wings keep a plane in the air. As the plane flies along, some air rushes under the wings and some air rushes over the wings. The moving air pushes the wings upward.

propeller

blade

The propeller needs to turn very fast to drive the plane through the air.

Engines power a plane through the air. This engine makes a **propeller** spin around. The propeller **blades** push air backward, making the plane go forward.

Old Planes

The first plane to fly using an **engine** was Flyer 1. It was built by two American brothers in 1903. They were named Wilbur and Orville Wright.

The Flyer 1 got into the air for 59 seconds on the fourth try.

People flew on this kind of airliner around 80 years ago.

An **airliner** is a plane that carries passengers. Early airliners were slow and very noisy. They were not very comfortable.

Where Planes Are Used

All planes fly in the air. On long flights, **jet airliners** fly about 6 miles (10 kilometers) above the ground. Some smaller planes fly closer to the ground.

Jet airliners fly above the clouds for long distances between cities.

The planes on the ground here are getting ready to fly. The plane in the air is about to land.

People get on and off planes at an airport. Airports are busy places with many planes taking off and landing. Planes take off and land on a **runway**.

Airliners

Passenger planes are called **airliners**. The Boeing 747 is a huge airliner. It is sometimes called a jumbo **jet**.

A jumbo jet usually flies between continents.

During the flight the passengers can eat a meal. Some jumbo jets even have video games in the backs of the seats for passengers. Jumbo jets fly on long journeys all over the world.

There are seats for hundreds of people inside a jumbo jet.

Amazing Planes

Supersonic planes fly faster than sound. Sound travels at about 750 miles (1,200 kilometers) per hour. Supersonic planes can go even faster! The Concorde was a supersonic **airliner**.

The Concorde flew very fast. On flights from Europe to New York, the plane could catch up with the sun.

The first trial flight of the Airbus
A380 was in 2006.

The Airbus A380 is the biggest airliner in
the world. Its two decks have seats for 555
passengers. It is made to fly very long distances.

Cargo Planes

A cargo plane is a plane that carries **goods**, or cargo. Inside the plane is a cargo **hold**. During the flight, boxes are tied down to stop them from moving around in the hold.

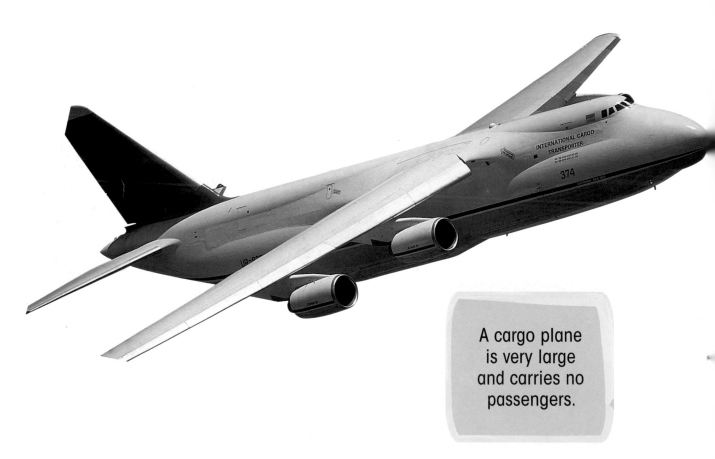

A cargo plane is very large and carries no passengers.

Cargo needs to be carefully packed and loaded into the plane.

cargo

A cargo plane has a huge door. It opens wide to let large pieces of cargo into the plane. A special truck lifts the cargo up to the door.

Seaplanes

A seaplane is a plane that takes off and lands on water. Seaplanes use the water instead of a **runway**. Seaplanes are useful for flying to places where there is nowhere to build a runway.

Seaplanes can land in areas that cannot be reached by car or train.

A seaplane has two floats instead of wheels.
The floats let the seaplane skim across the
water for takeoff and landing.

Seaplanes are like normal
planes on a pair of water skis.

floats

Vertical Takeoff

Some planes, such as the Harrier jet, can take off by flying straight up into the air instead of using a **runway**. The Harrier can also fly like a normal plane.

The Harrier jet is useful when there is not a lot of space to take off and land.

The power that pushes the Harrier jet upward also moves it quickly through the air.

nozzles

The Harrier has powerful **jet engines**. For takeoff and landing, the engine's **nozzles** point downward. For flying along, they point backward.

Gliders

A glider is a plane without an **engine**. A glider is towed into the air by another plane and then glides slowly back to the ground. People fly gliders for fun.

It can be relaxing to drift in the air through the countryside in a glider.

Gliders use the movement of the wind to go forward and to change direction.

A glider has long, thin wings. They keep the glider up as it flies slowly along. The glider's smooth shape lets it cut easily through the air.

Ultralights

An ultralight is a tiny plane. It can carry only one or two people. The wing is made of a plastic sheet that is attached to thin metal tubes.

An ultralight has a small engine and small propellers to keep it in the air.

24

The wing design and the pilot's skill keep this low-powered plane in the air.

The **pilot's** seat hangs underneath the wing. The pilot **steers** the plane up and down and to the left and right by moving a bar that is attached to the wing.

Fighter Planes

Military planes are used in wars to fight other planes in the air. They also attack targets on the ground. Fighters are small, fast planes that can turn very quickly.

This plane is known as the Eurofighter Typhoon.

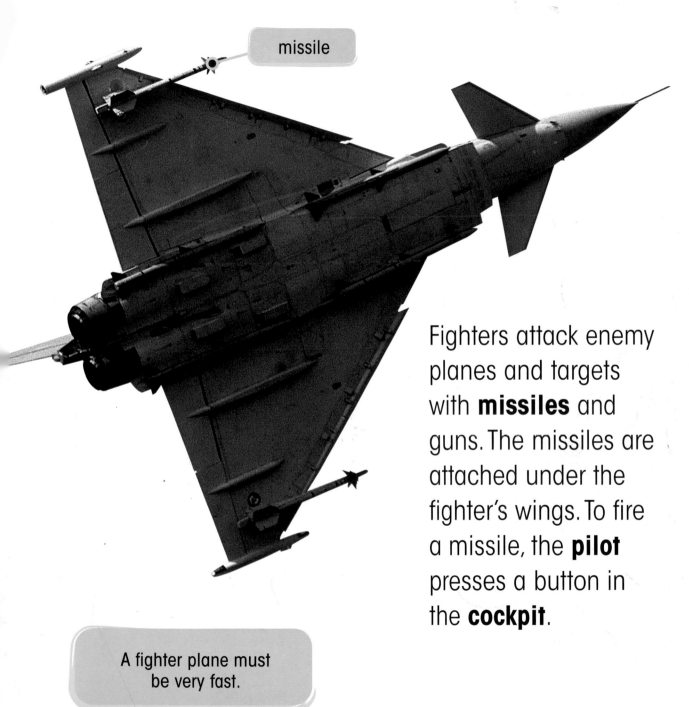

missile

Fighters attack enemy planes and targets with **missiles** and guns. The missiles are attached under the fighter's wings. To fire a missile, the **pilot** presses a button in the **cockpit**.

A fighter plane must be very fast.

Space Shuttles

A space shuttle is a plane that goes into space. It takes off like a rocket. Booster rockets give it an extra push.

space shuttle

The shuttle is attached to containers of fuel to help it into space.

When its job in space is finished, the shuttle returns to Earth. It glides down and lands on a **runway** like an ordinary plane. Parachutes help it to slow down.

parachute

The space shuttle needs an extra-long runway.

Timeline

1783   A hot-air balloon made by the Montgolfier brothers in France carries people into the air for the first time.

1903   In the United States, the Wright brothers take off in their airplane Flyer 1. It is the first airplane with an **engine** to fly.

1933   American pilot Wiley Post flies around the world on his own. The 15,500-mile (25,000-kilometer) flight takes almost eight days.

1969   The first Boeing 747 jumbo **jet** takes off for a test flight. Passengers first flew in a 747 in 1970.

1969   In France, the supersonic **airliner** Concorde flies for the first time. It starts carrying passengers in 1976. Concorde's last flight is in 2003.

1981   A space shuttle takes off for the first time from Kennedy Space Center in the United States.

2001   The Global Hawk flies from Edwards Air Force Base in the United States to Australia nonstop without a pilot. This is the longest flight ever by a pilotless plane, taking 23 hours and 23 minutes.

2005   Pilot Steve Fossett of the United States completes the first nonstop plane flight around the world on his own. The trip takes him 67 hours and 2 minutes.

Glossary

airliner   large plane that carries passengers

blade   one of the long, flat pieces on a propeller

cockpit   space at the front of a plane where the pilot sits

engine   machine that powers movement using fuel. A plane's engine moves the plane along.

goods   things that people buy and sell

hold   part of the plane where goods and luggage are kept

jet   one type of plane or engine. A jet engine sends out a stream of gas backward that pushes a plane forward.

missile   machine that flies through the air and explodes when it reaches its target

nozzle   hole where gas and hot air come out of an engine

pilot   person who flies a plane

propeller   part of a plane that is attached to the engine and turns to make the plane move

runway   long, straight strip of ground where planes take off and land

steer   guide the direction of a plane

Find Out More

Bennett, Leonie. *A Day with an Airplane Pilot.* New York: Bearport Publishing, 2006.

Millard, Anne. *DK Big Book of Airplanes.* New York: DK Children, 2001.

Tiner, John Hudson. *Airplanes.* Mankato, MN: Creative Education, 2004.

Index